What He Took

Also by Wendy Mnookin:

Guenever Speaks
To Get Here

What He Took

poems by

Wendy Mnookin

AMERICAN POETS CONTINUUM SERIES, NO. *71*

BOA Editions, Ltd. ❧ Rochester, NY ❧ *2002*

First Edition
02 03 04 05 7 6 5 4 3 2 1

Publications by BOA Editions, Ltd.—
a not-for-profit corporation under section 501 (c) (3)
of the United States Internal Revenue Code—
are made possible with the assistance of grants from
the Literature Program of the New York State Council on the Arts,
the Literature Program of the National Endowment for the Arts,
the Sonia Raiziss Giop Charitable Foundation,
the Lannan Foundation,
as well as from the Mary S. Mulligan Charitable Trust,
the County of Monroe, NY, Citibank,
and The CIRE Foundation.

See page 96 for special individual acknowledgments.

Cover Design: Lisa Mauro / Mauro Design
Interior Design and Typesetting: Richard Foerster
BOA Logo: Mirko

LIBRARY OF CONGRESS CATALOGING-IN-PUBLICATION DATA

Wendy Mnookin, 1946–
    What he took : poems / by Wendy Mnookin.
        p. cm. — (American poets continuum series ; no. 71)
    ISBN 978-1-929918-19-5
    I. Title. II. American poets continuum series ; vol. 71.

PS 3563.N66 W48 2002
811'.54—dc21

                                                    2002020803

State of the Arts

NYSCA

NATIONAL
ENDOWMENT
FOR THE ARTS

BOA Editions, Ltd.
Steven Huff, Publisher
Richard Garth, Chair
A. Poulin, Jr., President & Founder (1976–1996)
260 East Avenue, Rochester, NY 14604
www.boaeditions.org

Contents

Postcard from My Father   *9*

ONE

Map   *13*
I Refuse to Wear My Red Cardigan   *14*
How It Happened   *15*
Orderly   *16*
Intensive Care   *17*
This Is It   *18*
When My Father Dies   *19*
Shouldn't He Have Done Something?   *20*
My Father's Shopping List   *21*
Please   *22*
White Room   *23*
Ghost Flowers   *24*
Scar   *25*
Father's Glasses   *26*
The Girl on the Swing   *27*
First Aid   *28*
Ladder   *29*
Marooned   *30*
On Thick White Paper   *31*
Sunday School   *32*
What Lasts   *33*
The Booth   *34*

TWO

We Get Married Again   *37*
Matinée, 1953   *38*
Marshmallow   *43*
My New Father's Name   *44*
Perfumes Stare at Themselves   *45*
Mother in Her Black Lace Slip   *46*
Clues   *47*

Yes to the Father of Sweet Words   48
Love Story   49
Saturday Morning Cartoons   50
Rainy Day   51
Hives   52
Fontanel   53
Math   54
Polio Summer   55
This Is Only Practice   56
Dust   57
In the Girls' Room   58
Hiding Places   59

THREE

Desire   63
Annie Oakley Blows Kisses to Her Audience   64
How Men, How Women   68
Almost Egypt   69
Memory   70
Older Than He'll Ever Be   71
I Do Not Want to Long Always   72
Insomnia   73
Séance   74
I Can't Find His Obituary on Microfilm   75
Physician Is Fatally Hurt Near Abingdon   76
Finch, Waiting   78
His Fingers Vague as Wings   79
In the Garden   80
What He Took   82
Birds Are Carrying String Again   83
World Series: Boston, 1986   84
Let's Do It This Year   85
On the Anniversary of My Father's Death   86
Windows   88

Acknowledgments   90
About the Author   92
Colophon   96

for my fathers
and for my mother

Postard from My Father

—*March 29, 1949*

I hear you have a pretty red coat and hat.
I will be home soon
and give you a big kiss
and a present
and you can show me your coat.

ONE

Map

No matter what happens next
I want to remember
steam from an opened thermos of tea,
the smell of bananas,
a fold in the map through the center of Ohio.

You were two, you don't remember—

My father's glasses are falling forward on his nose.
He hums, off key, to the radio.
My mother's cheek is creased from sleep.

And the clothes, pressed
into the secrecy of suitcases.
I want to remember the clothes.

I Refuse to Wear My Red Cardigan

Let's just go—across the whole country
where there's another ocean

we'll swim in next summer. But we don't
even get to the star on the map

where my father promised we could stop
when the tires, tricked by rain, lose

the road. Wheels
hiss as they spin

in air.
            I'm over here

in a field by the side of the highway.
Look, veins

crisscross the back of a leaf.
I can slice them with my nail.

Why doesn't someone say something?
Click, click, the engine tries.

How It Happened

When my father feels the car
slide from the road and my body
rise from the seat as if beckoned,
he holds me back,
he lets his shoulders, the sweet
skin of his skull, slam the windshield.

~

When my father takes his eyes from the road
and his hand from the wheel,
when he reaches around to stop me—
Sit still!—from bouncing on the seat
and begging, again, for lunch,
the car leaps from its curve
into *sorry, sorry, sorry*, always
too late and not enough.

~

When my father's hands tighten on the wheel
I am in a kitchen seven states away
boiling eggs with my grandmother.
When they're done
she adds raisin eyes and lettuce skirts,
making the eggs pretty
so I'll eat them.
And still the road is slick.
Still, he fights the wheel.

Orderly

nuns swoop
into rooms where they make parents well
stretchers whine in the halls

and the orderly comes to me
his hair falls into his eyes

the orderly comes, he lifts me from the chair
and carries me to the water fountain
he makes his arms a sling around my waist
and holds me to the faucet, water

slaps my teeth like pennies

Intensive Care

My mother has climbed
to the top of a tall slide.
She's dizzy up there
where air is thin
and light stings her eyes.

It's too high for me to climb.
Hello! Hello!
I wait at the bottom.
I've lost a shoe.
I'm sucking my thumb.

> *Do you know where you are?*
> *Do you know your name?*
> *Tell me your name.*

My father can climb that high,
he doesn't even get dizzy.
He's climbed up
and he's slid down.
Now he's waiting.

What does he want her to do?

Holding tight to the handrails,
eyes clenched shut,
my mother backs down slowly
to where I wait,
one step at a time.

This Is It

He needs to think of what's important.
And so my father thinks of plums,
the small hard plums he found by the road
the summer he was seventeen
and biked through France. The first bite
was tart, almost bitter—
he sucked in his cheeks with surprise—
but somehow the next was sweeter.

When My Father Dies

First there's nothing,
a no-noise beyond silence,

and then a froth of white hisses in front of him,
hollowing out to a tunnel.
With a slap like waves breaking,

God's at the end of the tunnel,
Come to me, shrugging
a thin strap of night off one shoulder.

            But at the slip
in the whistle of my father's cells,
God turns his attention

to a striking mechanic in Center City.
Out on a picket line since 6 AM,
he scuffs the toe of his boot
and searches his pockets for a list,
what *was* the last thing?

Shouldn't He Have Done Something?

Did my father use the brains
that got him through med school,
smile the half-smile that won my mother,
did he strip off his clothes
and try to seduce God
with the twist and shine of his young body?

If that didn't work,
did he raise his hands
and claw red stripes down God's chest,
whatever it took, shouldn't he
have done something to stay with me?

My Father's Shopping List

—*September 14, 1948*

Cream
Milk
Butter
Eggs
Cottage cheese
American cheese
Coffee
Crackers for Wendy
Bread
Cold Cut
Oranges
Can Pineapple Juice
Baby Foods
    Fruits
    Veg.
    Meats
    Desserts
    Cereal
Lettuce + Tomatoes
Scouring Powder
Broom

Please

I want my father to forgive me
for twisting my hair around my fingers
and sucking the stringy ends
though I'd been told not to.

My hair tasted like the smell of me,
and the tired air of the car.

Don't tell me I was only two.
Tell me something
that will touch my father,
his palm up, as if asking.

White Room

White room with a single window
open to the breeze.

Room where simple food is served—
a plum.
A slice of bread.

A woman in white removes the tray.

Footsteps in the hall,
hum of machines whose names I don't know—
empty, ungrieving hours.

Always, the breeze.
And in my mouth, the taste of plums.

Ghost Flowers

Ghost flowers, my son calls geraniums
I carry from garden to basement,
where they wait through winter, stalks dry,

flowerless. When I was two, a nun held me
over my mother's hospital bed. *Look,*
she said, *look what you have to live for.*

None of them came up last spring,
my son complains. It's true. I watered them
for days and nothing greened. My mother

took a long time—her hair bloodied—
to raise her head. *Put me down,*
I didn't say, as her eyelids fluttered

at the nun's robe, her thin gold ring.

Scar

Mother parts her hair
and leans over
so I can touch the scar.
No, she says, *you don't remember,*
and goes back to making the bed,
snapping a sheet so folds spark.

But I can't stop remembering
a woman in a wrinkled skirt
who carried me to her car
and held me.

The ambulance came right away,
Mother says, pulling the corners tight.
There was no other woman.

The grasses were quiet.
The sky hung its wet curtain.
Maybe you should come with me, that woman said,
her blue scarf scratchy against my cheek.

Father's Glasses

Mother gives me his glasses.
They lie in my lap,
black frames with thick lenses
heavy against my thigh.

I pick them up.
This touched his nose.
This his temple.
Here it tucked behind his ear.

I put them on, look outside.
There, by the park, trees wave.
And in the window,
a girl, blurred, a little sideways.

The Girl on the Swing

Her father leans in with the weight of his body
and pushes
and she screams and her head falls back
and she sees him upside-down.

I don't like swings anyway.

I sit on the bench with my grandmother,
take my purse from the playground bag
and undo its shiny snap.
Comb, I say, not looking at her.
Penny. Mirror.
The objects pile in my lap.

Cookie.
We stare at the cookie
resting in its bed of crumbs.

First Aid

I'm at the beach in a ruffled swimsuit,
wrinkling my nose at the camera
in movie-star sunglasses,
showing off a sandcastle
with dripped-mud windows,
a seashell door.
I have a band-aid on each knee,

there's one on my grandmother's hand
as she waves at the camera.

And here's a child
long since forgotten—
see what I hold out to her?
A band-aid for her unhurt elbow
as she comes with her pail to play.

Ladder

The foghorn on the breakwater
sounds every thirty seconds,
a deep booming sound.
           —letter from my father to my
           mother, September 3, 1948

On the edge of my bed
Mother traces slow circles
on my back and shoulders,
hums bedtime words
like *stars* and *moon*.
It isn't mourning, exactly,
what we do together.
More like waiting
for the hour to settle
into its deep breaths.
Shadows grow manes,
invent tails. Tell me again
where my father is. And why
we call him *Richard*,
like a family friend
who's traveling
and doesn't have time to write. . . .
Stars gather themselves
into the shape of an archer,
I know that. I lie here,
open to any secret
that might slip
through the crack of the door
while the chair staggers its ladder
back against the wall.

Marooned

I'm tired of the sweet taste of coconut,
palm trees' brief shade.
Waves make me dizzy.

I've been here long enough.
Even my feet have toughened—
I walk barefoot on shells, without flinching.

And where is everyone?
I've tried and tried
but I can't teach the parrots to talk.

I want to go home.
Whatever I did
I won't do it again.

What if I send a message in a bottle?
Come get me!
written in berry juice.

Who knows where it will land,
if the boat's repaired.
Who will set sail.

On Thick White Paper

The teacher tells everyone to choose a state.
Kansas. I crayon
a farmhouse after a storm has swept through.

The walls shook.
Floorboards rattled.
Maybe the family went to the basement.

But you can't tell from looking at the house.
You have to walk to the field
and see the wheat.

Sunday School

If I die in second grade, will I spend eternity
practicing cursives, slanting my *l*'s
until they connect smoothly to my *y*'s?
Or maybe you can choose your age,
because otherwise heaven would be filled
with old people, smacking you wetly on the cheek
and telling you how you've grown.
I wouldn't choose seven, and neither would
Moses. He'd refuse an eternity
of helpless stammering, the jokes of other children
who'd pick him last for any game they played.
Karen would be seven, because she got to take the turtle home
for winter break, got to see that turtle
pull its head inside the dark window of its shell
and not come out till New Year's. And my father,
who died when he was twenty-seven, might choose
the summer he played stickball so late into evening
that his mother, leaning on the window ledge
until she chafed her elbows red, gave up
calling him in for dinner.

What Lasts

It's not me who peels
skin off the pudding
to get to the warm chocolate
thickening below. Not me
who lets the ball bounce twice
at jacks. I win if I say so.
Not my turtle scalded in the sink,
my library books piling in the closet
unreturned. Not mine, that
unkempt look, shoelaces dragged
in mud. Not my father
lying in the field, not his blood
puddling. Not my fault
if there was nowhere, nowhere
I could see, to get him a glass of water—

The Booth

I'll ride the merry-go-round if my father comes too.
I won't do the ferris wheel,
it climbs too high and sways at the top.
I want to watch it circle, arching my head back
till I'm dizzy. I want

a taste of cotton candy, a bite of hot dog,
a soda. I want to throw the soda in the garbage.
I want to sit on the bench
and take off my sneakers
and put them on again.
I want another soda

and I can have one
after we make a "happy birthday" record for my mother.
But the booth is too quiet, the red light
too red. I can't remember
what to say into the microphone.
And here's my father's voice,
tired, a little impatient,
Sing, Wendy. Sing.

TWO

We Get Married Again

This is the prettiest dress I'll ever have—
a satin sash ties in a bow, tulle swishes my ankles—

but Mother gets to stand with him,
their elbows touching, flowers

spilling over her hands,
while I sit in the first row with Grandma.

When he came to take her out
didn't I throw my arms around his neck

and kiss him, and didn't he blush,
from his forehead to his buttoned shirt?

I can hardly hear what they're saying
and when I ask, Grandma says, *Shhh,*

it's almost time to come home with me.
I don't like her parakeet, Pretty Boy.

I'll wrap myself in her velvet curtains
until I'm dizzy and it smells dark.

I love you, Wendy, Pretty Boy says.
He says that because she taught him.

Matinée, 1953

1.

My new father takes me to *Shane*.
Just me—my mother's afraid
of cowboys. The shooting.

I remember to take my rabbit's foot,
dyed blue, and when the lights dim,
when people stop rustling
and the lone cowboy rides in,
I reach in my pocket
and close my hand
around the cold, fur foot.

2.

Could a man
proud of his hat, creased just so,
a man who leans forward in his saddle, easy,
and smiles from under the brim,
could he be a cattleman
come to cut fences, trample
beans newly planted?

Joey's father stares at the rider
for as long as it takes
to draw two deep breaths.
Well, he thinks, *we could use
some help on the farm.*

3.

Dinner! Joey's mother calls, smoothing
hair from her eyes with the back of her hand.
Shane washes up at the pump
while Joey and his father
take their seats at the table,
the places they took the night before,
the places they expect to take tomorrow.

4.

When Shane's ax reaches
its highest arc, in the second it holds itself,
poised, in air, the father's ax leaps
into the stump. Chips
fly like bees, their pace
quickens. There's not a word
between them, just the *splat*
of iron on wood, the deep
pull of air into the body—
a V of sweat stains the father's shirt,
Shane's chest and shoulders shine—
until they set their axes aside
and throw themselves,
arms braced, against what's left
of the stump.

5.

The cattlemen start it
but Shane punches hard
and twirls fast
he knocks over a table
throws a chair
he can beat all of them

I love him
until two men pin his arms
and a third
smashes his fist across Shane's face
again and again. It's a long time

6.

before Joey's father storms in
to make the fight a little fairer—
the two of them
back toward the door together,
their eyes on the circle of men
who don't, for now, dare move.

7.

Joey's mother unpacks dresses from her trunk.
One is worn at the hem
where it dragged on the ground,
in another blue has bleached to grey.

Her wedding dress, fanned out
on the bed, still has every small button.

The wagon's waiting.
She must choose a dress,
one dress, and put it on.

8.

Couples move easily
into *step, step, point,*
hold, even Shane,
who dances with Joey's mother.

His father leans on a fence,
studies their dip and sway,
their turning. Shane's
spent so much time killing bad guys,
I can't imagine where he's learned to dance.

9.
There is the steady crying of the widow.
There is a hymn, words thinned
by prairie and mountains—*in life
and death, oh Lord, abide with me.*

There are women supporting the widow,
one on either side—
their coats are dark,
their skirts a faded blue, rose.
When the widow stumbles,
they grip her elbows more tightly.

There is *Dixie* on the harmonica
as men scrape the casket into the ground,
and, in the distance, smoke.
One of their houses is burning.

10.
Prairie grasses *shush* at their hooves.
A foal nuzzles a mare
and nurses. She nurses,
and the mare doesn't flick her tail
or turn her head. Harnessed
to a wagon, she's ready to pull it
wherever it is they're going.

11.
It'll be OK, Joey's father says,
before he rides into town
to settle things with the cattlemen.
His hands hang in his lap
like mittens drying on a stove.
If I get killed, he says,
you'll be cared for.

Outside, Joey waits
for him to say, *Shane,*
Shane will take care of you,
but all he hears is
coffee, cooling in a cup.

Marshmallow

A green stick bends
but doesn't break.
My new father cuts one,
strips bark in long curls.
With an army knife
that hides in his pocket,
he whittles the end to a point.

I poke at the fire, branches layered
so flames can breathe.
He wants to give me
an Indian name—
Tara-Wandala.

I peel off the char, too hot to eat.
Rising Sun, he says,
so sweet it's bitter.

My New Father's Name

Do you want to take your new father's name?
The judge's desk has feet
that stretch into claws
curling onto the worn wood floor.
He wears his smile like a party outfit
he doesn't want to wrinkle.

I want my new father's name.
I'm grown-up if I put *Miss* before it.
I wish there were flowers.
Is there going to be cake?

I want his name,
and I want to count the steps from the building—
forty-eight—
if my mother leaves me alone,
if she doesn't say a thing.

Perfumes Stare at Themselves

In Mother's mirror
brush and comb line up.
Hidden in drawers, slips
arranged by color, rows
of rolled stockings, camisoles
with straps so thin
they could break.

                    She sleeps
curled on her side,
my new father on his back.
His lips pull closed
when he breathes in, open
with a small *pop,*
a drop of spit.

                    I ease
the covers down, climb in
to be near him. In his sleep
he throws a leg
over my mother's hip.
The clock on her table
doesn't make a sound.

Mother in Her Black Lace Slip

She sways in circles around her room,
eyes half closed, arms reaching
to hug her own shoulders.
The radio scratches "Ain't Misbehavin'"
into late afternoon. She licks
a tear from her lip.

She should put on some clothes.
She should zip her skirt,
button the beaded sweater
lying now on the bed, one arm
flung toward the pillow,
the other hanging.

My new father will be home soon.

Clues

Shadows on the ceiling shift
as I listen, from my bed, for clues
to my mother's new life:
the bell-like thrum of a glass,
her laugh, a folded secret.
I listen so hard
I can hear my new father's hand
on the small of her back,
the sighing of her dress.

No words,
though sometimes the music of words.

When the lights click off
and their footsteps fade down the hall to their room,
I slide closer to the radiator.
If I'm lucky, voices
sputter thinly through the vents.

Do I hear *tomorrow?*
Does someone say *please?*

And why, at breakfast, does she lift—
slowly, and carefully,
with the tip of one finger—
a crumb of toast to her lips?

Yes to the Father of Sweet Words

Father of slim hips
Father of strong arms
painting the bedrooms
weighing the odds

Father whose pockets smell like smoke
hard candy, coins
asking to be counted

Father who carries me
above high dogs
Ha! I want to shout
but I just hold on

Father who wrestles me
to the ground
blows on my neck like a trumpet
stop, stop
until he doesn't

one father at work
one in heaven
which father will call to me
where's my sugar?
which father will come to me
home now, he's home

Love Story

I want the honeyed stare
my mother gives my baby sister,
curled like a comma in her lap. *Kiss,*

kiss, when she leaves for the movies
in one black shoe, one blue,
and just as quickly
comes home, but only to change.

I'm lucky, I can read in bed
until I'm tired, until words slip
from pages of *The Yearling*.
Do they want something from me?

In the morning my mother
opens my curtains, her hands
a hocus-pocus in lavender
and green. *Sleep well, sweetie?*

The light, a white surprise,
thins and thins, but doesn't tear.

Saturday Morning Cartoons

My sister sucks her thumb
and rubs her blanket across her cheek,
across the quick-changing flicker

from the screen. She's sleeping
so I tell her
We're not sisters.

Her face crumples.
We don't even have the same father.
Her eyes close tighter

than I thought they could,
squeeze out big, single tears.
It's not true, she dreams.

On TV, Popeye eats his spinach.
Muscles bulge from his arms—*boing!*
He's that strong.

My sister hiccups,
sucks her thumb harder.
OK, I say. *It's not true.*

Rainy Day

I'm the conductor
on chairs I line up
to make a train.
I sit in the first one
and go somewhere.

Out in the hallway
I stand by the mail chute
and wait for letters
to fall.

I open the phone book to *T*
and call *A. Tuttle*, tell her she's won a chance
to appear on "Queen for a Day."
She has the saddest story.
I have? she says.

I throw my dolls onto the coal roof
two floors down.
When their skirts billow out
it seems the air might hold them. . . .

They lie there,
Raggedy Anne's apron up above her head,
Charlotte with a twisted neck
and coal dust in her open eye.

Hives

Mother lies in my bed, knees up
to make a shelf, and reads to me
from *My Friend Flicka*.
The pink shine of her bathrobe
makes me shiver. In the afternoon

I get tea swirled with honey.
She drinks coffee, black.
The rash itches, but she doesn't want me
to scratch. *Think about something else,*
she says, kissing her lipstick to a tissue

as she leaves to pick up my sister.
I suck the bumps on the inside of my arm,
draw all the horses from *Let's Draw Horses*,
even the hard ones, running
and jumping over fences.

Fontanel

Elise Newman's baby brother
was born with a fontanel that didn't close.
I never asked why. We sat in her kitchen,
dangling our feet from stools,
and made shoe-shine kits from cigar boxes—
To Daddy, I love you in red.
It must have been Father's Day.
And I was happy, wasn't I,
to measure and cut Contac paper
just so, to glue on letters.
We had to be careful.

Math

My new father doesn't like it either.
He loosens his tie, unbuttons
three buttons at the top of his shirt.
Maybe he'll just have one cigarette—
he taps the pack against his arm,
leaves the others waiting in even rows.
Like this, he says, lighting up,
and crosses off a number in the tens column,
adds a tiny figure at the top.

When it's my turn
I swing my legs over the edge of my bed,
scuffing my slippers.
Paper thins under the eraser.
One number shoulders another
as he discovers I can't carry.

He breathes out slowly.
A perfect smoke ring
hangs over my bed.

Polio Summer

August of *The Secret Garden* we took turns
    playing Colin. If Ellen in her wheelchair
        was too tired, we pasted Trix on paper, orange boats

        on a blue sea, and always a sun, round and yellow
    and shining. The cereal coating mixed with glue,
smudged Ellen's face. When she got too sick

for us to play, no one wanted to be the invalid
    anymore, nursed to health with iced drinks
        and Milky Ways, although all she had to do

        was languish on the backyard chaise.
    The week before Ellen died, she floated
in a tube at the beach forbidden to us.

Mothers leaned together, whispered words
    we could never quite hear. What was it like,
        drifting weightless, legs sucked toward blue depths,

        face tilted to a white sky? Almost no one
    passed by our lemonade stand. Our fingers sticky
with syrup, and the salty taste of sweat.

This Is Only Practice

When sirens sound at school
we line up in hallways,
away from windows that could shatter,
desks that might collapse. Silent
and cross-legged, we sit
under blankets tented over our heads—
never look directly into that light.

It's good then to have a dead father.
When the bright light comes
he'll reach down, shadowing
my body with his,
and tie my shoelace.
He'll peel the covering
from a Cryst-O-Mint lifesaver
and hold it to me, saying

nothing. And he'll pick me up
and carry me, his hip thrust out
for balance, my hand tight
around the back of his neck,
the cool pulse burning my tongue.

Dust

Maybe the bomb has already fallen.
Maybe, as I brush my teeth,
as I walk to school, poisoned air
drifts my way. Mother says,
You're imagining things again,

but I see dust in the air,
feel it heavy on my shoulders.
Up and down the block
leaves are falling on yellowed grass.
There's half a worm under the swings.

Mother fixes chocolate pudding for dessert.
In *On the Beach* parents plan
how they'll dose the baby's milk
when the time comes, kill her quickly.
I'm not hungry, I say, and go to my room.

In the Girls' Room

I saw them making out, Sheila whispers
from the line of sinks. I imagine
her brother's hand surprising itself
inside some girl's sweater, small hairs jittery
along the map of her neck. *Her eyes were shut.*
I open mine wide. *She was making small noises,*
like a bird. I form my mouth into an O.
He was licking her ear. The bow of my breath
lingers, then disappears. I hate the ordinary
boredom of my life, my cotton underpants,
the sharp question of each hipbone. *Hey,*
she says, knocking on my stall.
I play with the lock, its silver tongue.
What's your secret?

Hiding Places

The story of a good girl begins with something
she doesn't want to lose—a sweater, beads embroidered
on the neck and sleeves. A lipstick, *Beach Plum.*

She never speaks of her father, the sharp brim
of his navy hat. Never tells how he gathered her
and whispered *kiddo,* like a prayer.

She still has the sweater. And the book of myths
with a picture of Odysseus tied to the mast.
Bound like that, what can he do but return home—

She turns the pages, whispering
Beach Plum as she runs her fingers through her hair.
Though the lipstick's been lost for years.

THREE

Desire

Some nights all I want
is the breath of our children catching
as they shift in sleep. The seed wings of the sugar maple
click softly against each other. In their rooms, the children
smell of hair damp from their baths.

                This is before
anything bad happens, because I have decided
there was such a time. If you want to touch me,
touch me.

Annie Oakley Blows Kisses to Her Audience

At first it wasn't a story,
it was my life gathering
under the trees, the traps
waiting, baited with corn.
Now it's always the same
grove of trees, windfall apples
packed away in straw.
I don't know anymore
if I dug sassafras roots,
my fingers stained, my mouth
watering for the first
sharp taste.
                    The gun
in my hand is heavy, then
light. There is glare and dust
and the idea BIRD
in the center of my aim.
Take me,
the rapid heart beats.

~

The sun sets, staining snow
the colors of a bruise, when a palomino
enters from the woods. She stops,
searching the air, then wheels around
and gallops north. I follow her
along icy streams, over granite outcroppings,
until she reaches the last canyon, perfect
for ambush. She throws back her head
and whinnies, races to my father

frozen in the wagon. I reach into my pack
for the Hudson Bay blanket,
but I wake, always, before
I can warm him, wool
clutched in my fingers.

~

When Mother cries at night,
quietly, behind her hands,
I know in the morning
she will set about her tasks early.

When she sits in the corner, staring,
her face stony,
I don't know her next move.

~

A grey sky,
two racing clouds.
My arms sting
though it's the rabbit
that scratches from the bramble.

The gift comes first, before
I squeeze the trigger.

~

He's seen the land across the ocean.
He likes me.
He can read and write.
He knows the stage.

I brush my hair 100 strokes,
sew flowers on my skirts.
I keep a mirror out
to practice smiling.
I rehearse my curtsy,
my kiss.
I marry him.

I go to sleep early,
keep my clothes folded
in the trunk, my guns
oiled and polished,
ready to go.

~
I shoot the clay birds
singly, in pairs, triplets,
four at a time.
I don't miss.

Do you love me now?

I shoot with my left hand,
I shoot with my right,
I turn from the target
and shoot with a mirror in my hand.
I never miss.

Do you love me now?

I shoot the ace of spades,
I shoot the ashes off a cigarette,
I hurdle a table

dive for my gun
pierce the thrown target before it lands.

I shoot
in quick succession,
bent on the record,
until the gun shines
red-hot in my hand.

Now?

I shoot
with stitches in my hand,
aiming and firing
until the stitches pull out.

Do you?

How Men, How Women

He wakes her in the middle of the night,
and says, Let's go all the way.
OK, she says, but soon

his breathing—and the small snore—
tell her he's asleep.
She watches

as the moon sifts
from one side of the room
to the other. In the morning

when she tells him, he says,
Oh, I meant, let's stay together,
you know, forever.

Almost Egypt

Locusts *ping* against our door
where two Jehovah's Witnesses stand,
trousers pressed, shirts tucked in.
Just tell them we don't want any, you call.
But they smile, earnest

as kindergarten teachers,
while they describe the end of the world—
mushroom clouds blossom
their delicate destruction,
milk glows blue.

When they leave I worry
about locusts, the way they fly into anything—
trees, lampposts,
people. Next
they'll swarm through fields, ravage crops.

This is New Jersey, you say.
I know the story—
hail, locusts, darkness.
The whine is growing louder.
Who cares if they're really cicadas.

Memory

I'll find it this time, barefoot, my breathing trained for surprise.
But when I round the tree it's disappeared into the gossiping of leaves.

Or the shadows have shifted and my husband
doesn't like the dog sleeping in bed, she twitches and moans
until he kicks her out. The shape in the covers is not the shape of a dog.

Is it that easy, just the imprint left, a little damp, a little warm?

Older Than He'll Ever Be

I'm here, rinsing vegetables,
where my father could find me
if he tried.

But he walks right by.

And do I care?
Butter's fuming in the skillet,
wild rice simmers in broth

while I peel an onion
down to its last thin layer—

he's curled in that onion
like a baby, naked
perfect, small.

I Do Not Want to Long Always

The baby slept in his crib, arms
splayed at his sides. He put everything

he had into this business of living—
his breathing earnest, serious.
His scalp smelled like grass,

or something else, something
I couldn't name, but knew even then
I would miss. My husband's whistling

was faint at first, but then louder,
clearer. That happy. When the child

grew older, I was greedy for solitude.
Come on, come on. Or was it
the almost-solitude of the sleeping child?

I slide a blade of grass between my lips.
The grass is sharper than I thought.
I worry the cut for days.

Insomnia

Where's your father? my grandmother asks.
In heaven, I tell her,
but she's not sure, or she's deaf,
and I have to keep saying it louder,
in heaven, he's in heaven,
which finally wakes my husband.
What? he says.
Where's my sister? I ask.
He pulls the pillow over his head.
*She's in New York, where do you think
she is?* Alabama.
I thought she was in Alabama
and I needed to send her sunscreen,
or maybe bug spray,
whatever it is they need
in Alabama. But that's my friend Joel
whom I haven't seen for years
and should call tomorrow,
if I'm not too tired, if the molecules
of empty chairs stay put.

Séance

You, in the yellow shirt.
Me? I'm not thinking of my father,
not concentrating
as we've been instructed.

A man, thin, taller than you, says
he knows you're having a hard time
and you're trying hard.

Having a hard time?
Trying hard?

After all these years
I want my father to find me
beautiful. Very smart. Very compassionate.

Trying hard?
This is ridiculous, I think.
That message could be for anyone.

And then: yes. It's for me.

I Can't Find His Obituary on Microfilm

—Public Library, Galesburg, Ohio

So my father isn't dead.
It's a story they made up
because he disappeared in the middle of the night,
taking only one suitcase.

Because he planned for months,
dividing, *his, hers.*
Because he had another woman.
Another child?

Come back, I know you didn't mean it.
Come back in late afternoon,
before the streetlamps come on,
so at first it's hard to tell

it's you, rounding the corner.
Older, yes, with grey hair
and a limp.
But still in your navy uniform

smiling a little sheepishly—
you know the story
you're about to tell
better be a good one.

Physician Is Fatally Hurt Near Abingdon

—Galesburg Daily Register,
June 27, 1949

Dr. Richard Reiss, 27,
was killed in an auto mishap
while en route with his family to the East.

> *it's the poem*
> *I need to write*

Mrs. Reiss, 26,
and their 2-year-old daughter, Wendy Ellen,
were passengers in the car.

> *the poem*
> *where I'm trying*
> *to be smaller*
> *on the stretcher*
> *next to his*

The auto he was driving went out of control
on Route 116, three miles west of the Junction.

> *the poem*
> *where I call*
> *to him*

Reports indicate that the Reiss auto skidded
after it struck a muddy spot on the wet highway.

somewhere
in the bundled
nerves of his brain

Dr. Reiss sustained a skull fracture
and crushing chest injuries.

he hears me—
his hand
flutters open, his fingers

He died in the Tarrant ambulance
on the way to St. Mary's Hospital.

uncurl
as if from the soft
fist of sleep

Finch, Waiting

At first, when he was getting used to being dead,
my father tapped on the kitchen window—

Over here! Over here!
Now he stamps on the porch floor

mostly out of habit.
I tie on my bathrobe, make the day's first cup of coffee.

If steam from his mug twists hieroglyphs across the door,
I don't need to read the message.

I know he's there. Eyes closed,
he holds the coffee to his face and breathes its heat.

But it's his fingers, his fingers are hard to watch,
laced so tightly around the cup.

The lawn is growing light, and the garden just beyond.
What kind of father is this,

who comes to me like a young lover?
A finch that's been waiting on the hemlock

skitters to the feeder.
I lean against the door. His knuckles whiten.

His Fingers Vague as Wings

I plant sticks in the garden,
tie them together at the top
for peas to climb.

I grate lemon for bread,
wring the oil onto sugar
while yeast bubbles in warm milk.
I add chocolate chips
so the children will eat it.

With the paper spread in front of me,
I sit on the kitchen floor
sipping wine. When I lean
against the fridge, humming
runs down my back.

In the sink, a blue bowl
waits to be licked, ceramic edge
chipped. I draw the shades,
shower until steam
sweats the bathroom walls.

In the Garden

I was pinching back suckers on tomato plants
and my daughter, who was two,
was digging in dirt beside me.
I was bent there, hidden, busy
making them perfect

when God said, *Stand*. I stood
and saw a purple Volkswagen, engine running,
painted peace signs dripping yellow.
A woman had one foot in our yard,
her hands on my girl's shoulders,

Where's your mother?
quietly, like she was sharing a secret.
When she saw me she fled,
didn't even get her door shut
before whoever was waiting gunned the engine

and they were gone.
I picked up my daughter
and pressed her too tightly to me,
tasting the sweat on her neck.
I didn't want to understand

my arms could be holding nothing,
with nothing to be done, no way
to go back and take better care.
But God said, *Stand*. God understood
a mother could be so absorbed in tomatoes—

neatly staked, well weeded in their even rows—
she wouldn't notice who had wandered from her.
When my father lost control of his car,
God was flicking sunlight into a gas slick
to see the colors flare.

What He Took

I kept the *shush* of sprinklers—
June was hot—and dogs sprawled
in neighbors' yards, but my father
took the possibility of hammocks,
the time of day he settled into,
or maybe it was night, the heavy
blanketing of stars. He shed
all gaudy particularities of adjectives,
the heft and shape of nouns, anything
funny he ever said. And the words
he yelled when he slammed the door
against—who? He took that too.

Birds Are Carrying String Again

My children have taken away their quick elbows,
their moods, their abrupt laughter.
Their feet don't rain on the stairs,
the jangle of the phone surprises me.

In the ebony silence, branches
outside the window tattoo
my closed eyes. Dusk
muscles whatever daylight's left
back to the end of the line.

I wanted my children to fill me up,
and they did
         or they didn't
and now, that's done.

World Series: Boston, 1986

One night's cold blackens the tomatoes.
The *Globe* prints a recipe for green tomato relish,
but it's too late. They've shriveled.

Tomato relish! I see my pantry shelves
lined with mason jars heaped with preserves,
sun glinting off glass, splintering

the green-gold harvest. Instead I pull vines,
stuff them into bags. I try not to think
of planting and watering, staking and weeding,

of Buckner as he bent to retrieve the ball,
then rose and slumped, arms heavy.
There was no need to hurry.

He missed a ball he must have caught
hundreds, maybe thousands of times before.
All the perfect catches, all the men tagged out

meant nothing up against the final score.
Why not think of Henderson's homerun
in the bottom of the ninth, one strike away

from defeat? As he danced around the bases
we stood and cheered, ready for a hero.
But my mind selects scenes for instant replay—

the missed ball, the ruined fruit.
Words I can't take back.
People I could have loved, or loved better.

Let's Do It This Year

Let's plant a plum tree in the backyard.
How many children did you want?
It's hard to remember. Once
they're here, they're here.
The children we'll never have
are the ones I love most,
especially at night, when the underside
of my eyelids exactly matches
the translucent skin of their fingers.
I don't know why I call you *Jimmy*,
that's a child's name. We should
go to Spain this summer
even though we don't speak Spanish.
If we plant the tree now,
how many years before we get plums?

On the Anniversary of My Father's Death

I lost my watch.
I had it for 18 years—
I took it to Minnesota when my son was 3.
I took it to Minnesota and to Maine,
to the top of Mt. Madison.
I wore it swimming in Echo Lake—it's waterproof.
I used it as an alarm each morning,
and on afternoons when I was reading and afraid
I'd fall asleep and miss whatever it was
I had to do next.

I was wearing the watch
on the outside of my left glove
so I could see it easily
when I was walking the dog.

It had an expandable strap
and the face was scratched.
You could press a tiny button and the face lit up.
At a movie, in an endless scene of
would-the-bad-guy-catch-the-good-guy
or would-the-good-guy-get-the-girl
I could press the button and see
how much time was left.

I didn't want another watch.
I wanted that one.
I retraced my steps
up the hill and around the school
and 4 blocks from home
I found it on somebody's lawn.

I don't know how
I happened to see it there.
But I remember
how sure I was it was lost
when I found it.

Windows

window of my room
where my father taped a picture of a snowman
the year there was no snow

hospital window
where my mother waved a red rose
so I could find her when my sister was born

windows overlooking a school
where each morning girls filed in
wearing blue jumpers and white blouses

studio window of my first apartment
with blinds angled to let in light

grates we mounted on eleventh-floor windows
though our baby was still too young
to reach the sills

windows of our house
which need washing
especially where the dog waits
pressing her nose

how you cannot see into windows
during the day, but at night
if lights are on inside

you can see everything—
the color of the paint
the wallpaper pattern
the ways people lean toward each other

Acknowledgments

My thanks to the publications in which poems first appeared, sometimes in earlier versions and with different titles:

The Antigonish Review: "Father's Glasses," "On Thick White Paper," "The Booth";

Boston College Magazine: "Almost Egypt";

Caprice: "Dust," "Marooned";

Chester H. Jones National Poetry Competition: "When My Father Dies";

Cimarron Review: "What Lasts";

The Comstock Review (formerly *Poetpourri*): "Fontanel," "Perfumes Stare at Themselves," "Polio Summer," "This Is Only Practice";

The Cortland Review (www.cortlandreview.com): "Let's Do It This Year," "Love Story," "Scar";

Hurricane Alice: "Annie Oakley Blows Kisses to Her Audience: *The sun sets, staining snow . . .*";

Kansas Quarterly: "Ghost Flowers";

New Millennium Writings: "Shouldn't He Have Done Something?";

Northwest Review: "Hives"; "We Get Married Again";

The Onset Review: "This Is It";

Oxford Magazine: "Mother In Her Black Lace Slip";

paragraph: "Windows";

Passages North: "In The Girls' Room";

Poet Lore: "Hiding Places," "I Can't Find His Obituary on Microfilm";

Radcliffe Quarterly: "Annie Oakley Blows Kisses to Her Audience: *I shoot the clay birds . . . ,*" "World Series: Boston, 1986";

Sandscript: "His Fingers Vague as Wings";

Stuff: "How Men, How Women";

Web Del Sol (www.webdelsol.com): "I Refuse to Wear My Red Cardigan," "What He Took";

West Branch: "Desire."

"Polio Summer" appeared in the anthology *Boomer Girls: Poems by Women from the Baby Boom Generation*, Gemin, Pamela and Sergi, Paula, editors, (University of Iowa Press, 1999). "When My Father Dies" (as "Before My Father Dies") and "This Is It" (as "Plums") were reprinted in *Poetry Tonight* (www.poetrytonight.com).

Thanks to the editors who recognized some of the poems with awards: "Shouldn't He Have Done Something?" (as "God And My Father on The Beach at San Pedro," *New Millennium Writings*, 1998) and "Ghost Flowers" (as "Wintering Over," *Kansas Quarterly*, 1994).

Thanks also to those who helped me hear these poems more clearly: Madeleine Blais, Anne Fowler, Abby Mnookin, Tam Lin Neville, and, especially, Barbara Helfgott Hyett and Elizabeth Kirschner. Thanks to Steve Huff and Thom Ward for their support and critical attention. I am grateful to my children, Seth, Abby, and Jake, and my husband, Jimmy, for love which makes the writing possible.

About the Author

Wendy Mnookin is the author of two previous collections, *Guenever Speaks*, a cycle of persona poems, and *To Get Here*, published by BOA Editions in 1999. A recipient of a fellowship from the National Endowment for the Arts, she has received awards for her poetry from *The Comstock Review, Federal Poet, Harbinger, Kansas Quarterly, New Millennium Writings, Poet,* and *prn.* In collaboration with Arts in Progress and the Massachusetts Cultural Council, she has taught poetry to children in Boston area schools. She has also taught poetry and creative writing at Boston College. She and her husband live in Newton, Massachusetts, where they have raised their three children.

BOA EDITIONS, LTD.

AMERICAN POETS CONTINUUM SERIES

No. 1   *The Fuhrer Bunker: A Cycle of Poems in Progress*
W. D. Snodgrass

No. 2   *She*
M. L. Rosenthal

No. 3   *Living With Distance*
Ralph J. Mills, Jr.

No. 4   *Not Just Any Death*
Michael Waters

No. 5   *That Was Then: New and Selected Poems*
Isabella Gardner

No. 6   *Things That Happen Where There Aren't Any People*
William Stafford

No. 7   *The Bridge of Change: Poems 1974–1980*
John Logan

No. 8   *Signatures*
Joseph Stroud

No. 9   *People Live Here: Selected Poems 1949–1983*
Louis Simpson

No. 10   *Yin*
Carolyn Kizer

No. 11   *Duhamel: Ideas of Order in Little Canada*
Bill Tremblay

No. 12   *Seeing It Was So*
Anthony Piccione

No. 13   *Hyam Plutzik: The Collected Poems*

No. 14   *Good Woman: Poems and a Memoir 1969–1980*
Lucille Clifton

No. 15   *Next: New Poems*
Lucille Clifton

No. 16   *Roxa: Voices of the Culver Family*
William B. Patrick

No. 17   *John Logan: The Collected Poems*

No. 18   *Isabella Gardner: The Collected Poems*

No. 19   *The Sunken Lightship*
Peter Makuck

No. 20   *The City in Which I Love You*
Li-Young Lee

No. 21   *Quilting: Poems 1987–1990*
Lucille Clifton

No. 22   *John Logan: The Collected Fiction*

No. 23   *Shenandoah and Other Verse Plays*
Delmore Schwartz

No. 24   *Nobody Lives on Arthur Godfrey Boulevard*
Gerald Costanzo

No. 25   *The Book of Names: New and Selected Poems*
Barton Sutter

No. 26   *Each in His Season*
W. D. Snodgrass

No. 27   *Wordworks: Poems Selected and New*
Richard Kostelanetz

No. 28   *What We Carry*
Dorianne Laux

No. 29   *Red Suitcase*
Naomi Shihab Nye

No. 30   *Song*
Brigit Pegeen Kelly

No. 31   *The Fuehrer Bunker: The Complete Cycle*
W. D. Snodgrass

No. 32   *For the Kingdom*
Anthony Piccione

No. 33   *The Quicken Tree*
Bill Knott

No. 34   *These Upraised Hands*
William B. Patrick

No. 35   *Crazy Horse in Stillness*
William Heyen

No. 36   *Quick, Now, Always*
Mark Irwin

No. 37 *I Have Tasted the Apple*
Mary Crow

No. 38 *The Terrible Stories*
Lucille Clifton

No. 39 *The Heat of Arrivals*
Ray Gonzalez

No. 40 *Jimmy & Rita*
Kim Addonizio

No. 41 *Green Ash, Red Maple,*
Black Gum
Michael Waters

No. 42 *Against Distance*
Peter Makuck

No. 43 *The Night Path*
Laurie Kutchins

No. 44 *Radiography*
Bruce Bond

No. 45 *At My Ease: Uncollected Poems*
of the Fifties and Sixties
David Ignatow

No. 46 *Trillium*
Richard Foerster

No. 47 *Fuel*
Naomi Shihab Nye

No. 48 *Gratitude*
Sam Hamill

No. 49 *Diana, Charles, & the Queen*
William Heyen

No. 50 *Plus Shipping*
Bob Hicok

No. 51 *Cabato Sentora*
Ray Gonzalez

No. 52 *We Didn't Come Here for This*
William B. Patrick

No. 53 *The Vandals*
Alan Michael Parker

No. 54 *To Get Here*
Wendy Mnookin

No. 55 *Living Is What I Wanted: Last Poems*
David Ignatow

No. 56 *Dusty Angel*
Michael Blumenthal

No. 57 *The Tiger Iris*
Joan Swift

No. 58 *White City*
Mark Irwin

No. 59 *Laugh at the End of the World:*
Collected Comic Poems 1969–1999
Bill Knott

No. 60 *Blessing the Boats: New and*
Selected Poems: 1988–2000
Lucille Clifton

No. 61 *Tell Me*
Kim Addonizio

No. 62 *Smoke*
Dorianne Laux

No. 63 *Parthenopi: New and Selected Poems*
Michael Waters

No. 64 *Rancho Notorious*
Richard Garcia

No. 65 *Jam*
Joe-Anne McLaughlin

No. 66 *A. Poulin, Jr. Selected Poems*
Edited, with an Introduction
by Michael Waters

No. 67 *Small Gods of Grief*
Laure-Anne Bosselaar

No. 68 *Book of My Nights*
Li-Young Lee

No. 69 *Tulip Farms and Leper Colonies*
Charles Harper Webb

No. 70 *Double Going*
Richard Foerster

No. 71 *What He Took*
Wendy Mnookin

Colophon

The publication of *What He Took* was made possible
by the special support of the following individuals:

Debra Audet
Laure-Anne Bosselaar & Kurt Brown
Daniel & Elissa Arons
Nelson Blish
Susan De Witt Davie
Carol Cooper & Howard Haims
Marsha & Michael Freed
Dr. Henry & Beverly French
Dane & Judy Gordon
Kip & Deb Hale
Peter & Robin Hursh
Robert & Willy Hursh
Dorothy & Henry Hwang
Jennifer & Craig Litt
Carla Lynton
Anne Lenox & Jim Sersich
Boo Poulin
Deborah Ronnen
Jane Schuster
Pat & Michael Wilder
Stephen Wilson
Sabra & Clifton Wood

This book was set in Monotype Dante
with Adobe Woodtype Ornaments
by Richard Foerster, York Beach, Maine.
Cover design is by Lisa Mauro / Mauro Design.
The cover painting, "Road to Raymond"
by Keith Jacobshagen, is courtesy of the artist.
Printing was by McNaughton & Gunn, Saline, Michigan.

Printed in the USA
CPSIA information can be obtained
at www.ICGtesting.com
JSHW082223140824
68134JS00015B/702

9 781929 918195